The Golden Crossroads

A MYSTERIOUS JOURNEY

JAKE McCREA

◆ FriesenPress

One Printers Way
Altona, MB R0G 0B0
Canada

www.friesenpress.com

This is a true story based on real event and characters. It's a testimony of the author's evolving faith, as a result of his experiences before and after the crossroads. He shares his life, portraying the mania and depression of a bipolar mood disorder, and describes his destiny to emerge spiritually reborn and grounded.

ISBN
978-1-03-917592-1 (Hardcover)
978-1-03-917591-4 (Paperback)
978-1-03-917593-8 (eBook)

1. POETRY, CANADIAN

Distributed to the trade by The Ingram Book Company

Prologue

As a musician and poet, I took off for Vancouver to start a new life. I had just finished a university degree after returning from an epic journey through Europe a couple of years earlier. After slugging it out in the big city for a couple of years I reluctantly travelled back to Saskatoon for an interview to further my education. I returned to the coast with my best friend to consider the future. It was a hitch-hiking journey we would never forget.

A spiritual quest turned into a test of survival as we came face to face with the devil at a crossroads in Golden, B.C. I was forced to face my own mortality and stare death in the eye. A trip through Hell followed. A cascade of strange coincidences leads me to believe I was responsible for saving the world, but ended with me getting committed to the psych-ward and diagnosed with a bipolar mood disorder. I was forced to deal with my own personal demons on my road to recovery.

I met a lot of interesting people on my journey to mental stability and spiritual enlightenment. My quest for the meaning of life continued and eventually I accepted the signs and the reality that God exists. Faith and fate collide in my crazy adventure through the crossroads and beyond as I searched for truth, a life purpose, self-identity, and peace of mind.

After successfully learning to manage my mental illness, getting free from my dependency on alcohol, and after decades of meditation and reflection, I documented my story in this collection of songs and poetry. Following the straight and narrow path to sobriety, and through the saving grace of God, I hope to inspire others that time heals all wounds, peace is possible, and redemption is close at hand. All it takes is a little faith to open the door to a more meaningful life.

Jake McCrea
September-2021
Saskatoon

Table of Contents

Chapter 1. 1
European adventure (1989-1990)

Chapter 2. 13
Vancouver life (1993-1995)

Chapter 3. 25
The crossroads (1995)

Chapter 4. 35
Through Hell and back

Chapter 5. 53
Searching for love in all the wrong places

Chapter 6. 67
Alcohol and idiots, the devil's grip

Chapter 7. 77
The desire to live righteously

Chapter 8. 87
Giving thanks and seeking redemption

Chapter 9. 97
Truth, prophecy, and the celebration of life

Chapter 1

European adventure (1989-1990)

Stringless Kite
London Busker
Mountain High
Doomsday Ride
Black Market Money
Sundown

STRINGLESS KITE

Starting off with all the blame
Wild hearts are hard to tame
But listen child, it's now to claim
Tomorrow's too late to seize the day
Some they smirk but it makes me laugh
Only shadows on my brow-beaten path
Telling tall tales to entertain
Who's to judge what's sane or insane?

Let's take time to fly away
Reach the sky before we die
Let's take time to leave today
Life's too short to live a lie

Experience a shining star
Open dreams, distant, far
Buried guilt, discovered light
Defying limits
Stringless kite

Choose your path and who's to say?
A little luck may come your way
Take the highroad to eternity
Shed some light on the uncertainty
So when they tell you it can't be done
Tell them you're probably the only one
Life is sacred in its destiny
A bitter sweet tale of reality

Let's make time to fly away
Life's too short, heed the call
Let's make time to leave today
Roll the dice and break the fall

LONDON BUSKER

By twilight the sounds were clear to my ears
Music originating from somewhere near
Familiar was the song
Unmistakable guitar and vocals along
To '*Hotel California*' in the fall
I was warmed to the soul by it all
On a cobblestone street for a pint of ale
Pubs on every corner in a festive scale
People casually walked around
Seeking out that '*Eagles*' sound

The busker was a one-man band
As he entertained the streets
We all gathered to listen to his rendition
As he attempted this feat
Under a street light near a quaint park
The busker stood performing his art
People threw coins in his case
As did I, I was so amazed
I admired his talent
And respected his profession
He loved what he was doing
You could tell by his expressions

Shook to the core, never before
Had a song sounded so pure and alive
Influenced me more
To someday learn to sing and play like that guy
To master the guitar before I die

What a cool way to pay the bills
Playing guitar and living the thrills
Like the busker in the London square
I didn't know fate would take me there
But something evolved from that moment on
Into a love for creating poetry and song
Something got a hold of my curiosity
And I turned it into destiny
Just like the busker over seas
I was meant to be my own company

Shook to the core, never before
Had a song sounded so pure and alive
Influenced me more
To someday learn to sing and play like that guy
To master the guitar before I die

MOUNTAIN HIGH

In Innsbruck I picked up some bread, and cheese
And a cheap local wine
I was going for a hike up the nearest peak
But I didn't leave much time
I marched up the rugged pass
Sometimes it got downright scary
Eventually crawling on all four limbs
And my wine was hard to carry
But I kept going till I found a sanctuary
A view of the Austrian panorama
A perfect place to drink and dine
Photos with my camera

It could have been the altitude
Or the beauty all around me
But why I got so smashed
On the local wine confounds me
I felt destiny had brought me there
And I thanked God for that moment
But now I had to descend the beast
My final opponent

Life wasn't going to get better than this
It was all downhill from there
I was a rolling and tumbling mess
Down the mountain as dusk drew near
I was running out of light
As the sun was going down
And I was running out of time
To find my way back into town
Cause I was mountain high Lord
On a mountain high

I didn't tell anyone where I was going
I could have fallen off a cliff
No one would have even known
That I would have been a miss
Looking back I realize
Life was truly won
I had it all, I philosophized
As I raced against the sun

I want to get that feeling again
It's been 30 years or so since then
Hopefully someday
I'll be that content
An inner peace
And sense of accomplishment
I still have photos to remind me
Of that moment in time
I let it define me
Never far from my mind

DOOMSDAY RIDE

Flagged down a beat up van
Hitching at night from Florence, Italy
Three sketchy looking dudes
Opened the back doors for me
My gut instinct told me to pass
But I was desperate for a lift
It could have been my last

I decided to jump in the back
After a little hesitation
One guy slammed the doors, locking them shut
Too late to have reservations
The van was a prison cell, dark, cold, and dirty
Only a sliding glass window separated the cab from me

But I took a chance with some hillbillies
Now I'm trapped in this cell and it's killing me
I've got to get off this doomsday ride
Before it ends in potential homicide

I crouched near the window sitting on my heels
Carefully observing my foes
I realized they were all wasted
As we swerved all over the road
On cold steel, moving left and right
Losing my footing, fearing for my life

Creepy dudes with crazy talk
Like little school girls they giggled and mocked
As they described what they proposed to do.
I pretended I didn't have a clue
I took out a steak knife and was prepared to use it
If they veered off the freeway I was going to lose it

There was one way to avoid impending doom
I had to be persuasive, because a bleak fate did loom
I pleaded that I'd buy them coffee at the next truck stop
They looked reluctant but agreed to a shot
When they pulled up to a truck stop they let me out
I grabbed my things and left them standing about
"Ciao my crazy amigos, no café tonight!"
I was relieved and feeling alright
They just got in the van and rode away with nothing to say
A huge weight was off my shoulders
A crazy ride which made me grow a little older

BLACK MARKET MONEY

Budapest in the fall of '89
Things were tough and treating me unkind
Hitched my way from Vienna in the rain
Getting a ride was a viscous thing
But I arrived all tired and wet
And my spirit wasn't broken yet
I needed money to get me some food
Then it occurred to me out of the blue
The black market rate was probably a steal
More bang for the buck, a full meal deal

Looking to trade in the downtown square
I approached a guy who gave me a stare
"Change money?" He spoke from the side of the scene
"Yes!" I said as I passed him some American green
Just then a clean cut guy, who looked like a cop
Grabbed me from behind, telling me to stop
Together we split in opposite ways
No time to check the bills that he gave
And I ran out of luck since the deal went funny
Cause the son of a bitch ran off with my money

What goes around comes around
Or so they say
You rob me of my money
You're destined to pay
Karma has a way of working things out
I was going to get even, without any doubt
Getting ripped off is a hell of a thing
When black market money is only a sting

The thieves left me bills from a fractured economy
Now I was left with a bitter feeling inside of me
I knew I wouldn't see my money again
But maybe I could shake up my black market friends
I figured the two were working together
Playing the law was all pretty clever
Expectedly I saw them talking under the lights
I guessed that's where they plotted their heists
Walking from behind, I gave them a shove
I snapped their mugshots and told them, "Talk to the judge!"

What goes around, comes around
Or so they say
Smile for the camera
It's your lucky day
I'll plaster your face across town
So the authorities know you're lurking around
Getting ripped off is a hell of a thing
When black market money is only a sting

JAKE MCCREA

SUNDOWN

On the rocks as the sun was sinking into the ocean
I sat in peace as waves crashed relentlessly
Against the shore below
I could hear the pounding of my heart
I could feel the brisk wind through my hair
Last rays of light sent tingles down my spine
Thoughts could not enter my mind
Nor emotions fix upon my face
Beauty seemed to hypnotize me
Leaving me with nothing, but peace

The hours came down to minutes
In every minute
I was the entire focus of the earth's seduction
Suddenly a cool breeze
Sent chills through my body
And a cold anxiety woke me
As the sun went down over the ocean
No longer was I the center of the universe
So I got up from the cold rock
And I walked away

Chapter 2

Vancouver life (1993-1995)

Suspended
Vancouver Nights
Poetry In A Bottle
My Mistress Mary Jane
Very Lucid Time (into the cryptic tank)
Street Licks
The Kerouac Song
Delirious Beats

SUSPENDED

(David Morgan/Jake McCrea)

Suspended
No way up, long way down
Suspended
Travelled far, can't seem to get my roots out of this town

Traffic's steady but the city moves slow
Hold the frame, roll the picture slide show
Times are changing, destinations I chart
But nothing is sacred if there isn't a heart

Days in bloom, but I can't see you
Days in bloom, but I can't hear you in this room
Everything changes with time, cut the line
Everything changes with time, cut the line
Could the best be left behind?

Suspended
One step ahead, two steps behind
Suspended
No fast-paced town could get you out of my mind

Traffic's steady but the city moves slow
Hold the frame, roll the picture slide show
Times are changing, destinations I chart
But nothing is sacred if there isn't a heart

Days in bloom, but I can't see you
Days in bloom, but I can't hear you in this room
Everything changes with time, cut the line
Everything changes with time, cut the line
Could the best be left behind?
Suspended, Suspended
Suspended in time

VANCOUVER NIGHTS

I was pumping fists with a fellow derelict
The night was a complete mess list
From the junkies to the heretics
I was mingling with all sorts of strangers
In dark alley doorways
Just looking for a little danger
Just daring the night away

Living out the midnight moon
Far into the morning sun
Play me just one more tune
Until another Vancouver night is done

I was trying to make peace in a land of confusion
Offering an ear and a heart to an old man's delusions
I was playing my cards in the game of life
And this is what the dealer, he dealt me tonight

All the best at my request
It's nothing less than a mysterious quest
Karma comes, and we're just like dharma bums
And that's the way we passed the days
The city's cruel when you're the fool
To have success you must impress
Living free with destiny
Through the ruthless streets I beat
Across the Vancouver lights at night

POETRY IN A BOTTLE

(Donald Burke/Jake McCrea)

I drink alone, I drink in my room
My pad is my own once again
No one in my face once again
Is this good or is this bad?
To answer this I must go mad

Misplaced words, forgotten thoughts
That's the life that we have sought
But through these pages we must turn
And like a candle we must burn
Like a candle we must burn

Sunny sky but lonely night
To be alone would be a fright
Passing out at 7:30
Alcohol is definitely dirty
Yet I continue in this sin
Although I know I'll never win
Nor did I write '*Ode to a Nightingale'*
But I drink JD and ginger-ale

Another drink, another poem
Another girl, another thought
Waiting for a phone call
Looking for influence of the bottle
Drink myself into oblivion
All alone in my pavilion

MY MISTRESS MARY JANE

It's time to give my mistress Mary Jane a rest
Enough is enough God knows I gave her my best
Don't think I can handle
To live out a scandal

Mary Jane
My mistress Mary Jane
My mistress Mary Jane
My mistress Mary Jane

I'm a man in need of some clean air to think
But when I'm without you my mood starts to sink
I can't flirt with desire
Just adds more sticks to the fire

The same groans from a desperate cast
It's the same stones as I lie in the grass
I thought last time you'd change my mind
But as before you're just a whore
But it's the same stones
That keep me coming back to you

Just leave me like you've raped my mind
With a fake clown's mask and wasted time
But you're the talk of the town
You get myself unwound
But you're not my mind

VERY LUCID TIME (into the cryptic tank)
(Jake McCrea/Matt McCrea)

And it's a very lucid time
Now my backs against the wall
And all the tales they do unwind
Just like writing on the wall
And I can't accept the fall
No I can't accept the fall
And it's a very lucid time
I stand staring down the hall
Now I know I must decline
Before I lose it all
And I can't accept the fall
No I can't accept the fall

Just when I think I may have won
Double looney never comes
Can't save the rest for the bank
So I shot another blank
Into the cryptic tank
Into the cryptic tank

And it's a very lucid time
As I walked away from the scene
And the crowd looked so divine
But their manner so obscene
Wish my pockets weren't so deep
Wish my pockets weren't so deep
And it's a very lucid time
Cause I only lost again
And the pain is always mine
And it all goes back to when
When I had to start again
When I had to start again

STREET LICKS

The nights were mine
I thrived in the dark
Back alleys and neon signs
Strolling through the park
I saw it all playing street licks
Met a wide range of holy beatniks
From small-time crooks on the run from the heat
To dharma bums with their sacred beliefs

Busking in the sky-train at the central station
The epicenter of a beat generation
When up barged a junkie as white as a ghost
Proclaiming that he overdosed
Fresh from the hospital and looking to kill
The guy who sold him the lethal pills
Brandishing a knife he wanted directions
But 'accessory to murder' didn't sound good on reflection
So I said I was new to the city
And didn't know my way
But for the guy I felt pity
As I wished him better days

I was playing outside a Richmond liquor store
When three long-haired dudes stopped to hear more
Sitting on a bench across the road from me
They were a peculiarity
They asked me to join their band
After a brief audition
"You are '*Domino Theory*' now", they said
Like I didn't have a decision
Then I met them on the road, way up north
But they canned me when I didn't know all the chords
The idiots didn't know what rehearsal was for
And I had to play songs I hadn't heard before

On a beach in the west end of town
Entertaining strangers as the sun was going down
A young guy heard me playing 'Brown-eyed Girl'
And said it sounded great
Came back later with a tape recorder
Wanting a rendition for his date
He said he was going to use it to propose
She was the girl of his dreams
I was honored to assist
As strange as it all seemed

There were many other stories
And many other memories
Street licks paid the bills
And made a slice of history

THE KEROUAC SONG

Jack Kerouac was funny man
With the stories he told
He went up and down America
Life on the road
It was okay that life was hard as nails
He made it sound so good
Jack wrote religion
And man! The hippies understood

I want to be a hippie to
I don't want to work like others do
Just give me a guitar and let me write
A song that would inspire you
Cause me and Jack are tired
Of doing things that we don't want to do

Dean Moriarty in 'On The Road'
Didn't seem to worry about anything
He was as reckless as can be
But I have to say I liked him
Dean had the philosophy that life could be rich
And exciting all the time
He seemed invincible but in real life
He like Jack died before his prime

Jack knew what's true and good in everyone
Tried to make out that life could be something fun
But Jack why did you lose the inspiration
That was all a part of you?
I believe you had a sacred message
And I wish you only knew

I want to be a hippie to
I don't want to work like others do
Just give me a guitar and let me write
A song that would inspire you
Cause me and Jack are tired
Of doing things that we don't want to do
When you're doing, something you don't want to do
When you're doing, something you don't want to do
When you're doing, something you don't want to do

DELIRIOUS BEATS

(David Morgan/Jake McCrea)

Bring arguments that can't be proven
Echo a voice around the hall
Send guitar across the basement
Splash paint against the wall

Some things just can't be spoken
Some dreamers remain asleep
Look around the corner
And bide your time
Delirious beats

Bend out the edges, blur the time
Wrap the floor in canvas, sample fine wines
Jamming beats go on and on
Like putting poetry to song

Flashing cameras in the night
Get a grip and hold on tight
Find what's lost but never found
Reach for the sky and leave the ground

Chapter 3

The crossroads (1995)

Magic Door
The Old Man
On A Moody Day
In The Midst Of Destiny
On The Road To Golden
Take Me From The Crossroads
A Home Of Dreams

MAGIC DOOR

The autumn sky had fallen, cold, damp, and dusty blue
Another stranger reached to me and you
Who was this disguise? Portrait of times
"Please realize", he shrugs
"I'm down on my luck, so could you give a little up
For a poor man?"

The autumn sky was calling
I can remember, I can remember
The autumn sky was falling

The lines on his face were beaten
Told times of misery
You could see the scars run deep beneath his words
"On this street I'll sleep, dream on my feet
But thanks a lot for the silver for thought"
Said the poor man

The autumn sky was calling
I can remember, I can remember
The autumn sky was falling

As I watched the dying sun
My shoulders cold and numb
I want to give you so much more
Wish I had a magic door
Wish I had a magic door

THE OLD MAN

The old man grips you like a vice
His words inspired with advice
"Don't waste your time consumed by wealth and self-pride"
And in his words I do abide

The old man stops a second for a song
And he wants to sing along
"Drink a toast to all the dreamers of the past
In this spirit they will last"

Just like the old man used to have
The rainbows pot of gold
Life was a plan on behalf
Of a truth he never sold
Gave me the cross around his neck
And he prayed that I wouldn't forget
And lose my way

The old man holds his confidence inside
And in his prayers, I would rely
"May the Lord protect and guide you through your day
As you're playing on the sidewalk stage"

ON A MOODY DAY

The mood today is a product of our thinking
We need some love to keep the raft of life from sinking
But I know it's just a matter of time
The mood today will awaken us from sleeping
We'll change our ways and be grateful for believing
In ourselves when life gets us down

It's okay to get lost in thoughts that confuse you
No one knows your life like you do
But we get caught in the tide
When there's nowhere left to hide
We're blind, on a moody day

The mood today all depends on how your feeling
Some days are great, while others leave you reeling
But in the end there's just peace I'm sure

It's okay to get lost in thoughts that confuse you
No one knows your life like you do
But we get caught in the tide
When there's nowhere left to hide

We're blind
When we try to walk the path of life
By using feelings
Blind
But there's an end to the uncertainty
Can you seal it?
Blind
Like a ship amongst the waves, we drift around some days
Peace of mind is hard to find, when you realize you're blind
But whenever you're distressed, you can think of how you're blessed
Then you'll know for sure, there will always be a cure
There will always be a cure, on a moody day

IN THE MIDST OF DESTINY

Sending a postcard from yesterday's fool
Talking the wild times, breaking the rules
Playing guitar on the corner for dimes
Writing out pages like footprints in time

Someday I'll grow up
Growing true to you
Someday I'll give up
The need for all the clues
Somewhere in the midst of destiny
Somewhere in the midst of destiny

Reading the headlines, only the trash
Kicking up dirt from the ground on my path
Listen for angels, will they leave the signs?
Praying for God and the prophets in time

In the midst of destiny
I see the crossroads ahead of me
Feels like I'm losing my sanity
Carry me, carry me
In the midst of destiny
I hear a voice within me
Show me the way and comfort me
Sing to me, yeah sing to me
In the midst of destiny
In the midst of destiny
In the midst of destiny

ON THE ROAD TO GOLDEN

On the road is where I lost my mind
I was looking, cause I had to find
A link to what's real
Why I feel this way?
It didn't take me long to believe
Hell's angels were coming for me
But I could feel it in my soul
I'd never be sold on damnation

On this road is where we stand
Hitching our way to the Promised Land
Memories are like castles in the sand
But we won't be lost again
And I'm grateful for a friend
On the road to Golden
On the road to Golden, on the road to Golden

Travelling along by thumb can be tough
Especially if your friends had enough
But we made it through the door
Just like before we were moving
Blessings come in strange disguise
And I'm not lost in simple goodbyes
Cause no one ever leaves
If you believe they inspire

Something's got my soul, and it won't let it go
On the road to Golden
I can't find my way, so this is where we'll stay
On the road to Golden
I won't tell a lie, and I won't let it die
On the road to Golden

31

TAKE ME FROM THE CROSSROADS

Just like a prophet would teach
Gave us a ride and began to preach
It will come true
Revealed to you
The demon's face
A lonely place

The cloud approached from the sky
And I was thinking I was going to die
Like a race
Between time and fate
A baby cried
I wondered, why?
Is life a game to be won?
Please Lord, take me from
The crossroads

I heard the story of Kingdom Come
But I can't die like His only Son
I'm just a man in agony
Why do you bring me to my knees?

We'll sleep by the river tonight
We'll have to sleep or we'll die of fright
But I'm too cold
And I sold my soul
Where's my guitar?
It can't be far
Is life a game to be won?
Please Lord, take me from
The crossroads

I heard the story of Kingdom Come
But I can't die like His only Son
I'm just a man in agony
Why do you bring me to my knees?

The only way out was by bus
And then the tickets were given to us
But don't get off
And there's my Prof.
He'll write the story
We'll live in glory
Is life a game to be won?
Please Lord, take me from
The crossroads

I know the story of Kingdom Come
And I'm going to die to overcome
The demon's face in front of me
Now I know it's my destiny
Now I know it's my destiny
Now I know it's my destiny

A HOME OF DREAMS

It seems like such a long time since we talked
And we were just thinking about you
How you been doing? Everything's fine
And I'm spending my time at ease
Yeah, I'm spending my time at ease

Tell me where are you going?
Cause we care about you
Tell me what you've been doing?
Cause we love you
Please come back to visit
But I can't find my way
So it's just another lonely day

When the sun goes down tonight
I want to sleep in peace and recite
A dream inside my head
And make my home in bed instead

I'm still walking down that same back-alley deja-vu
Shall I listen to me or confide in you?
I'm feeling the blues, but everything's cool
I just need you to understand
I need you to understand

Tell me where are you going?
Cause we care about you
Tell me what you've been doing?
Cause we love you
Please come back to visit
But I can't find my way
So it's just another lonely day

Chapter 4

Through Hell and back

Moody Days
Jacob's Ladder
Keeping The Devil At Bay
Jake Jr.
Flight From Hell
The Funny Farm
What The Hell Is Hell
Tales Of Empathy
Out Of The Dark
When A Lonely Heart Pleads
Something In The Way I Feel

MOODY DAYS

Moody days are following the blind man
Star-crossed generations walk behind them
The young echo cries of confusion
Greed's bent on demise, built on illusion
While our thoughts into the tide

We're blind
And our homes cut out of the hills
We're blind

Moody days will awaken us from sleeping
Eclipsing ways to keep the pulse of life from dying
You raped and you stole for your waste
Left scars on the face of the future
While our thoughts into the tide

We're blind
And our homes cut out of the hills
Forever leaving, blind
And it seems that only moody days can change our thinking
Blind
Exploitation for the debt, will time tick till nothings left?
Who will be giving us our bread, after everything is said?
But to you I must confess, I don't have all the answers yet
Peace of mind is hard to find, when you realize you're blind
Forever leaving, yeah we're blind
Forever leaving

JACOB'S LADDER

A stairway to Heaven
A Greyhound through Hell
Wrestling angels
Cast in a spell

Riding into the Promised Land
With everything intact
Mercy seemed to take our side
I didn't think we'd make it back

A vision of evil
A fate worse than death
Selling my soul
To pay off my debts

Riding into the Promised Land
On a bus ride through Hell
On the alter of sacrifice
But now I live to tell

Dealing with the devil
He said he'd take my life
Unless I sold him my soul
"You'll be a legend despite"
So I said, "I don't know!"
Jacob's ladder is the road to redemption
Somewhere between Heaven and Hell
Jacob's ladder is a scary descension
To my knees I fell
And the devil wants me to sell

Greyhound bus tickets for two
A one-way trip through Hell
On a mission to save mankind
So others may live to tell
The secret to the signs
A legend so divine

Dealing with the devil
He said "You're doomed to fail,
To Hell with the rest!"
But my will would prevail
As I'm forced to face death
Jacob's ladder is the road to redemption
Somewhere between Heaven and Hell
Jacob's ladder is a scary descension
To my knees I fell
And the devil wants me to sell

Accepting my fate
And my desire to live on
I thought I'd dedicate my life
To making up for my wrongs

Riding into the Promised Land
With my rider at my side
Thank God we made it!
To the place where I reside
To my pad on the west side

KEEPING THE DEVIL AT BAY

The devil's weight on my shoulders and I'm taking the hits
Rolling with the punches, losing my wits
The devil's weight on my shoulders and I'm ducking for cover
Desperate to see, seek to discover

Keeping the devil at bay
Is a load off my shoulders
No more sins to repay
And a little bit bolder

The devil's weight on my shoulders and I need some more time
Eager to act, looking for signs
The devil's weight on my shoulders but there's one way out
Lay down your life and continue the bout

Keeping the devil at bay
Is like quenching a thirst
No hunger or plague
A total rebirth

The devil's weight on my shoulders and there's nowhere to hide
Lay down by the river, rider at my side
The devil's weight on my shoulders as I carry this pack
Full of sin and pain, trade it all back

Keeping the devil at bay
At the scene of the crime
This evil I must delay
Or have I run out of time

JAKE JR.

Jake Jr. in hand and out of my head
Everything else I had lost on the way
A Jasmine Takamine, in a starburst red
It was as beautiful as it was to play
I abandoned Jake Jr. in Abbotsford, B.C.
Coincidentally, the home of my birth
All on account of what prophets foresee
And a mission to save the earth

Into the bush Jake Jr. was thrown
And I was off and runnin'
Now I'd reap what I had sown
And the devil was'a comin'

Jake Jr. made me tons of money
Paid for itself a thousand times over
Was instrumental in picking up the honeys
Like the charm of a four-leaf clover
But now Jake Jr. was out of luck
My life was doomed to self-destruct
Jake Jr. was just dead weight
I wouldn't let this decide my fate

Into the bush Jake Jr. was thrown
And I was off and runnin'
Now I'd reap what I had sown
And the devil was'a comin'

The devil was hot on my trail, looking to do me in
I was bound to fail, drowning in sin
The angels were down, and I couldn't read the signs
Evil was all around, and I was running on borrowed time

41

FLIGHT FROM HELL

On the run with nowhere to turn
A payphone out of the blue
A collect call to my family back home
I needed someone to talk to
Under the gun with no way out
I thought about ending it all
I was having some serious doubts
And no further could I fall

Phoning home to salvation
Hoping someone's there
A refuge from damnation
The only ones that care

On the phone as a cop arrived
She said she'd stay with me for a while
I was just surprised to be alive
My mind was in denial
All at once the taxis pulled up
Each of them offering a ride
So I jumped in the first one I saw
And he drove to the west side

Paranoia strikes again
Hell's angels are after me
Had I gone completely insane?
Or was this my new reality?

I stayed with a friend that evening
He picked me up at my pad
My flight didn't leave till the next morning
I tried to forget that I had gone mad
At the crack of dawn we were off to the airport
And my friend walked with me to the gate
Pinned a small angel to my collar
And I made for my escape

Flying on wings of paranoia
Trying to catch my breath
Just stay on the plane and don't get off
It was a matter of life and death

A flight from Hell to destiny
Away from the grips of the devil
The time I spent in agony
Was about to get back on the level
A flight from Hell to eternity
To the safety of my home
My soul was returned to me
And now the seed is sown

I made it to Saskatoon by the grace of God
And my parents were there to greet me
I felt relieved but it struck me as odd
When they took me straight to emergency

THE FUNNY FARM

Committed to the funny farm
Staring at the ceiling
Wondering just what the hell happened
The nightmare left me reeling
Under security of the pod
A place where all lost angels go
All I did was think I was God
Nobody told me it wasn't so
But the doctor said,

"These meds will help you focus your mind
You'll do better if you take them with time"
I didn't believe him but the doctor was right
Reality slowly came into clear sight

Committed to the funny farm
But the signs kept on coming
This was no coincidence
I knew it was meant for something
My roommate in the pod had a similar story
A trip through Hell and back
Feeling the pain and the glory
Facing the devil, under attack
And the doctor said,

"These meds will help you focus your mind
You'll do better if you take them with time"
He didn't believe him but the doctor was right
Reality slowly came into clear sight

Avoiding conversation, tormented by signs
My roommate and I kept our distance
But I couldn't help noticing, the similarities were stunning
What we experienced we knew in an instance
It's no fluke we both received an angel pin from a friend
Or that we were both reading the same books of prophecy
But we also continue to write about our stories
On the path to recovery

"And they think we're crazy!" we would say
Mocking the doctors and the meds that they gave
But eventually in time my mind became clearer
As I began to recognize the face in the mirror

WHAT THE HELL IS HELL

What the hell is Hell?
I can't begin to tell
Off of the rock I fell
My soul to sell
What the hell is Hell?
Cursing the wishing well
All evil is propelled
To the ringing bell

What the hell is Hell?
What the hell is Hell?

What the hell is Hell?
In a world of pain
Nothing to gain
Nothing remains
What the hell is Hell?
When there's no one to listen
Everyone's busy
Everyone's missing

What the hell is Hell?
With nothing to eat
No room for a bed
No shoes on your feet
What the hell is Hell?
With no belief
No questions to ask
No answers to seek

TALES OF EMPATHY

Tell a tale that will empathize
Call it a favor for a lonely guy
Make it sad so that I feel it inside
But give me hope in the other side

When I sit here disengaged
And the storm begins to rage
I can't stand how the rain
Is driving me insane
I lose my senses, I feel defenseless
Because I know you'd die for me
Tell me tales of empathy

There was a man who testified
From his sins he could not hide
But his faith he kept alive
Until the day he died

As I pray and meditate
The clouds begin to break
Then a rainbow paints the sky
Just like that the storm subsides
But my loneliness remains

OUT OF THE DARK

I can't see the sunshine today
The clouds cover the sky in a dark display
I'm just thinking, I think I'm sinking
Is there another way?

Everything's going wrong
I can't bear to sing along to nothing, no nothing!
And though I'm in despair and thinking life's unfair
A shadow of myself, don't mean the words that leave my mouth
A shadow of myself, don't mean the words that leave my mouth

No one can blame me today
No need to dwell over yesterday
Life's not a race, and I'm tired of the chase
God only knows the long road it has been
And I can admit, I couldn't resist
Guilty of another sin

But now I'm going strong
And I can sing a song for something, yeah something!
I want to let you know God cares and He feels the cross you bare
And in the end I know, I'll pray to God to save my soul
In the end I know, I'll pray to God to save my soul

And the sun broke through the clouds
I felt my heart beat fast and loud
God was a man, the truth maintains
He's calling out my name
Out of the dark again and again
Out of the dark again and again
Out of the dark and losing my shame
Out of the dark and staking my claim
Walking a path of promise to fame
Out of the dark and finding my way
Out of the dark and learning to pray
Shedding some light on a long moody day

WHEN A LONELY HEART PLEADS

Dreams never die is only a lie
When time has left them behind
Fighting the fears and holding the tears
Only to comfort the mind
Praising the dead and things that are said
May give to someone who needs
But nothing has changed of all that remains
And only this lonely heart pleads
What's this fall in me?
Will I be set free?

Watching the years, the face in the mirrors
Reveals a window to the past
Loosening skin, a grain in the wind
The sail gives way to the mast
A ship on the water or a lamb to the slaughter
Knowing all channels must end
Parting the play, breath from the day
With all the others descend

Take the stage that silenced me
This old news won't carry me
Pierce the dark that drags me down
And my heart begins to pound
Take the stage that silenced me
This old news won't carry me
Pierce the dark that drags me down
And my heart begins to pound
What's this fall in me?
Will I be set free?

Take the stage that silenced me
This old news won't carry me
Pierce the dark that drags me down
And my heart begins to pound
Take the stage that silenced me
This old news won't carry me
Pierce the dark that drags me down
And my heart begins to pound

What's this fall in me? Will I be set free?
When a lonely heart pleads
Take the stage that silenced me, this old news won't carry me
When a lonely heart pleads
Pierce the dark that drags me down, and my heart begins to pound
Another lonely heart is found

SOMETHING IN THE WAY I FEEL

Younger years seemed to tumble
And my dreams they were left to be sold
Still I'm waiting for a sign
How will my life unfold?

The best of times
In the worst of minds
Yeah, the test of time
I can't be wrong, it's something in the way I feel
I will respond, it's something in the way I feel
Until that something fades away

Hiding for cover in my own beaten self
Waiting for my world to turn
I guess we all have a cross to bear
As we watch the candle burn

The best of years
In the midst of tears
Pacify my fears
I won't break down, it's something in the way I feel
I'll stand my ground, it's something in the way I feel

How long?
How long till I find my peace of mind?
How strong?
How strong do I have to be to get over the past?
And carry on, yeah carry on

Chapter 5

Searching for love in all the wrong places

Who Was This Angel
Nice Girl
Innocence Lost In life
Stay On The Ground
A Sad Song On A Hot Summer Day
Sheena Said
The Dreamer
I'm Crazy For You Sue
Ex (once upon a lie)
Don't Deceive Me
Missing Link

WHO WAS THIS ANGEL

Who was this angel?
Angel of the morning or of the night
Only to a complete stranger
Would she cut you like a knife
Who was this angel?
She'd make you remember
Your fall from grace
That night in November
And she's the pretender

Who was this angel of the night?
Come with me, seduce me
Angel of the night
Use me, abuse me

But who was this angel?
I was warmed by her smile
Forgive my intrusion
But could you talk for a while?
And who was this angel?
She'd make you forget
A night of sin
And all your regrets, you can bet

Who was this angel of the morning?
Refresh me, console me
Angel of the morning
Invite me, delight me

When an angel comes with render for your soul
You may surrender to the demon in us all
But when an angel comes to bring you compassion
That's when you finally get some satisfaction

NICE GIRL

I thought she was a nice girl
Man! Was I mistaken?
Welcome to the free world
All my dreams forsaken
At the MGM Grand, on the Vegas strip
One more spin to win and she blew me a kiss
She came to me with that look in her eye
"Back in a minute," she said with a smile

Then she walked away with a stranger
It was kind of hard to understand
A little money could change her
And she gave up on demand

She came back without her friend
About a half an hour later
She said she had a job to tend
Someone else to cater
Things just got worse when she dropped the line
"I'll charge you of course, if you take up my time"
Then I got the hint, an angel's demise
Not surprising her looks were just lies

Then she walked away with a stranger
It wasn't hard to understand
She liked the thrill of danger
And her looks were second hand

I thought I met a nice girl, when promise led to nothing
You know you're out of luck when the only chick around is bluffing
Lady of the night! Leave me alone to gather the pieces .
Remains of my self- esteem, why do you deceive-eth?
Oh! And I thought she was a nice girl

"I've got kids to feed and bills to pay
It's how I make a living
Just need your cash to stay
For the attention you'll be given"

Then she walked away with a stranger
It wasn't hard to understand
I guess you couldn't blame her
She just used the desperate man

I thought I met a nice girl, when promise led to nothing
You know you're out of luck when the only chick around is bluffing
Lady of the night! Leave me alone to gather the pieces
Remains of my self-esteem, why do you deceive-eth?
Oh! And I thought she was a nice girl

INNOCENCE LOST IN LIFE

Innocence lost, haze set over the hills
Well nothing will change as the child drifts into the pills
Paranoid delusions, the remains of the past
Sweat from a nightmare, she awakes in the midst of a gasp

Grin and strut a smile
Merchandise to buy and sell
Used goods are reimbursed
Daddy's girl won't die a curse, no!
When she, when she's forced to walk the plank
And everything is blank
Another innocence, lost in life

Sink into the night from her window to the street
Racing through a poisonous shelter to cool the stifling heat
Deep under passion or product of greed
Left for the Mercedes yuppie to feed

Doing a trick, she was laid on the ground
One sorry family that couldn't, wouldn't whistle a sound
Private Violet opened twice a day
Once for the road and once for the people who prey

Sweet little crumbling leaf
Shattered off a fallen tree
Broken through once again
Maybe never live till when, no!
The light will come to shine and mend
Over steepened hills and bend
Reflections on this picture frame
Innocence, another innocence
Innocence lost in life

STAY ON THE GROUND

She thought the world would see
A candle in the storm
And all she shared with me
Was all the pain she was adorned
She wore the thorns
Ever since the day she was born

She thought the world would see
A lost soul in distress
And all she wants to be
Is to be different than the rest
She always tried to impress
She never got that depressed

Hey girl! Hey girl! Don't let me down
Hey girl! Hey girl! Stay on the ground
Hey girl! Hey girl! Karma comes round
Stay on the ground

She thought the world would see
Her jumping from a ledge
And all she said to me
Is she'd be better off dead
With angel's voices in her head
She clings to life by a thread

Many men must have treated her wrong
But she's strong and she wants to belong to someone
I know that life is a gift, so it's time to get rid of it
The drugs will only bring you down
So come on girl, stay on the ground

A SAD SONG ON A HOT SUMMER DAY

Don't know who I want to be
Don't know what I want to do
Don't know where I want to go
But I'm lonely inside

Don't know what I should believe
Don't know what is right or wrong
Don't know what life has in store
But I'm lonely inside

And I'm dying to meet someone
And I'm burning on a trail to the sun
Cause no one seems to come my way
It's a sad song on a hot summer day

Don't know why you don't like me
Don't know why you complain
Don't know if what I say will hurt you
But I'm lonely inside

Don't know when the time is right
Don't know if you want to hear
Don't know why you are so special
But I'm lonely inside

SHEENA SAID

I met Sheena outside her door
She was locked out on the second floor
So she waited in my suite for a while
I was taken by her innocent smile
Together
Then we talked into the night
And things they seemed to go just right
Sheena made good love in bed
But I never knew what went through her head

Sheena said, Sheena said
Sheena said, Sheena said

Sheena said I was a creepy old man
She liked to tease me like a fun girl can
Sheena said that 30 wasn't too old
She was barely 20 with a heart of gold
However
Sheena's love didn't last long
In some way all the spice was gone
Sheena went back to her boyfriend past
Somehow I knew it wouldn't last

Sheena said, Sheena said
Sheena said, Sheena said

I got caught in the feeling
Came off much too strong
If only I knew
She only needed a friend
So it ends

Sheena said, Sheena said
Sheena said, let's be friends

JAKE MCCREA

THE DREAMER

And there's life inside this man
Yeah, something's got me by
Because I know I always can, try again
Try again, at meeting a friend
Try again, at meeting a friend
And there's a girl I used to know
Yeah, she was a real gem
But as the saying always goes, you can't be friends
You can't be friends, if it's all pretend
You can't be friends, if it's all pretend
So I tell myself and I tell myself

It's time to be alive
Shake your blues until you're free
And it's time to be alive
You always said to me
Sing a sweet song
Because I know you'll always be
The dreamer to me, the dreamer to me

Now I dream for hours it seems
Waiting for a clue
Will you come and join the team, just me and you?
Just me and you, so my loneliness is through
Just me and you, so my loneliness is through
So I tell myself and I tell myself

It's time to be alive
The wind will catch your sail
And it's time to be alive
You'll walk along the rail
Sing a sweet song
Because I know I'll always be
The dreamer to me, the dreamer to me

I'M CRAZY FOR YOU SUE

Crazy, for a girl named Sue
Crazy, what will I do?
She's only seventeen
Doesn't have a clue
But her eyes they see me through
She's a wild one
With a sweet smile
But she's only a child
Still it's hard to care
When the attitude is there

Sue, I want you
The others won't do
I'm crazy for you Sue

Crazy, for a girl named Sue
Crazy, what will I do?
She's a real fox
When she ties up her hair
I want to be there
She always wears a skirt
On that tiny little frame
Man! It drives me insane
But Sue won't get flirty
With an old man of thirty

Though I know Sue's too young for me
I want to see her desperately
She's the only one that can light my fire
Watch the flames burn higher and higher and higher

EX (once upon a lie)

A king stood proud in long thin halls
Naked, starlit, free
Pondered on an outcast knight
Lonely soul was he
Myth, and tale, and folklore ride
On wings of destiny
To curse the perfect Aphrodite
And mock her history

Too naive and weak are we
The past has come to Deities
She lurks the halls of misery
Terrified to witness Thee
She's ex, once upon a lie

Bloody swords and willowed roses
Wasted hate to ride
Purely golden thoughts of two
Left to drift the tide
Convincing mask of the goddess
Makes royalty of pride
But pockets deep with rotten tricks
Once upon a lie

Too naive and weak are we
The past has come to Deities
She lurks the halls of misery
Terrified to witness Thee
A knight is all he wants to be
Lock the goddess, throw the key
Ever after's all it reads
And happiness a memory
She's ex, I'm ex, we're ex

DON'T DECEIVE ME

Hidden teardrops in the rain
Concealing bitterness again
There was a hope that we would be
But then you steal it like a thief

You took the sunlight from the day
And then you hid it in your cave
You shook all the stars from the sky
And robbed the vision from my eyes

Don't, don't, don't deceive me baby, don't
Don't, don't, don't deceive me baby, don't
Don't, don't, don't deceive me baby, don't
Don't, don't, don't deceive me baby

Say I'm a drifter with a lost sail
Say I'm a poet with a sad tale
Perhaps I'll see you in my dreams
And there you'd love me like it seemed

MISSING LINK

Sunday afternoon drinking to clear
All these thoughts of my dear
I feel lonely and it's painful to think
Of all that went wrong and my missing link
I used to walk down by the river at night
With my sweet little girl just holding me tight
And it's sometimes a wonder to think
How I'll get by with a missing link

Was it destiny?
Or an entity?
That vanished like a spark from the flame
Thought I'd believe
When you said we'll be
Together till the sun burns out
Why, did I see you despise?
When the look in your eye proved it was all built on lies
My missing link

Yesterday's answers were today's demise
Nothings left sacred in a pack of lies
The pieces of the puzzle just didn't seem to fit
Everything was ruined so I decided to quit
So now the bond linked us no more
As I grabbed my jacket and headed for the door
Today it's just a wonder to think
How I'll get by with a missing link

Chapter 6

Alcohol and idiots, the devil's grip

Criminal Relations
The Great Beating (Humpty's last crack)
My Demon Alcohol
A Smooth Reputation
Ignorance And Arrogance
Radio Bites

CRIMINAL RELATIONS

Have I bit too much to chew?
When I'm bending backwards to assist you
And you dis my integrity and blessing
It's hard not to hate when you're the lesson
I'll hang no more with a pompous fool
Leave through the front door, shake off my shoes
A lot of love is all that's missing
And this jerk needs a total revision

Give a little, take a little
It's all in reason
But don't abuse my right of being
It's just criminal relations
Share a little, care a little
Friendships for the giving
But don't abuse my right of being
It's just criminal relations

When God came down it was to save
Now it's time for us to behave
If disrespect is all you share
A life of torment you will dare
It's not to say I'm unforgiving
But to the brink I have been driven
Especially when an ego collides
And takes you for a one-way ride
Through Hell, so long pal!

I should have learned the first time
You disrespect and treat me unkind
Go back to where you came from
Stick a fork in our acquaintance, I think it's done
Well done!

THE GREAT BEATING (Humpty's last crack)

I went to a lounge one night in Saskatoon
Three musicians were on stage, two of which I knew
One played guitar, a childhood prodigy
The other played bass at my CD release party
But it went off with a hitch when the bouncers got mad
And my face needed stitching cause it ended really bad

Smashing through the window
Looking for a beating
Opening Pandora's Box
On the curb and bleeding

It was a bad idea to bring beer inside
Because I couldn't disguise my stash
I could sense their well-trained eyes
And they were looking to kick some ass
They hurled me through the entrance window
The goons they had me pinned
The smashing of glass as the beating continued
Punishing blows to pay for my sins

Smashing through the window
Looking for a beating
Opening Pandora's Box
On the curb and bleeding

Now I know how Humpty Dumpty felt after he had his great fall
I knew he would crack if he fell off the wall
And all the king's horses, and all the king's men
Would scramble to put us together again
Oh, what a shame, the great beating is to blame

Lying on the curb all scrambled and beaten
Here comes the cops, and I knew I was defeated
Off to the drunk-tank where I knew I'd be sleeping
What a place to spend the weekend
When I awoke I was a complete mess
Hangover and all I was in terrible distress
My face stuck with blood to the concrete floor
My eyes and lips were swollen and sore
Black and blue I must have stolen the show
What have I done to assume such a role?

Yeah! I played the clown alright
And the monkey wrecking crew wanted the fight
Guess who's the laugh in town tonight?
The boy's in the band probably cringed at the sight
My thoughts were on the bridges I burned
Oh God! When will I ever learn?
I think I'll quit drinking till respect can be earned
Until then I'll adjourn

MY DEMON ALCOHOL

My demon alcohol
My demon alcohol
When things are rough, they'll only get rougher
My demon alcohol
When I want to cure the pain, I call it by name
My demon alcohol

When I want to splurge on a gambling urge
My demon alcohol
When I hit the hard stuff, I never get enough
My demon alcohol

It's insane the time I wasted
Drinking to forget the past
And all the trouble it caused
From the first drink to the last
This demon has a grip on me
So now it's time to set myself free
No longer will I live in shame
With no one but myself to blame

My demon alcohol
My demon alcohol
When I'm feeling on top, the harder I drop
My demon alcohol
When I act like an idiot, the ladies aren't into it
My demon alcohol

When I have regrets over something I said
My demon alcohol
When I cause a scene by acting obscene
My demon alcohol

The cause and solution to all life's problems
At least that's what I entertained
But alcohol's the gateway drug
And it's time to end this risky game
That's why I left it all behind
Cause now I see the guiding signs
Things started to come around
I just had to put the bottle down

A SMOOTH REPUTATION

A smooth reputation is hard to maintain
When you need booze for the nerves
A little confidence to entertain
Because when you're out on stage
And you don't get a fix
It's sometimes hard to go through with it

Lord, give me the guts and the grace
To entertain in any place
A smooth reputation is what I require
A smooth reputation so I can get hired

A smooth reputation is all about class
But the cynical spectator has his head up his ass
Everyone's a critic and it gets on my nerves
Especially when you're playing to serve
Get up here and show me your stuff
If you think you'd do better, I'll call your bluff

I want to have the confidence to hit the stage
Without all the crap that gets in the way
Because you're only as good as your last show
That's just what I've always been told
So when you get a chance at redemption
Carry on a smooth reputation

IGNORANCE AND ARROGANCE

It's just ignorance and arrogance
You think you're a rock-star
You're not even a musician
It's significant to my defence
You won't go far
If your ego makes decisions
You're not a producer
You have no credentials, don't know potential
You're a complete loser
A serial abuser
No honorable mention

It's just ignorance and arrogance
You like to play judge
You think you're better than others
It's significant to my defence
You're stuck and you won't budge
I don't know why I even bother
So get off your high-horse
And join reality, have some empathy
It's time to divorce
I know I can't force
An enemy

You think you're rich and living the dream
But your life's a bitch, never to be redeemed
Riding on the coat tails of other's success
And your criticism is meaningless
Ignorance in what you say and do
And I'll always know you're just an arrogant fool
I'd be surprized if you have a single friend
And you missed your chance to make amends

RADIO BITES

I'm lonely, only, song plays, today
It sucks, more bucks, for them, so then
I sigh, goodbye, so long, I'm gone
Hey you, won't do, I learn, to turn
Anybody got a disc to play?
You know I'm tired of this stuff they say
I need a groovy tune to keep me going
I need a special sound to keep me from slowing

Radio bites
In the still of the night, when I thought it might in spite
Show a little style
Radio bites
In the break of the day, they got nothing to say, got nothing to play
Could someone turn the dial?
Radio bites, radio bites

Song ends, God send, I'm glad, too bad
Forsake, to take, the pain, insane
Mainstream, bad scene, to play, or stay
Tuned in, listen, to this, mischief
Anybody got a disc to play?
You know I'm tired of this stuff they say
I need a groovy tune to keep me going
I need a special sound to keep me from slowing

I like something a little more hip
This really bites and I'm sick of it
I guess I'll just have to turn this crap off
So pull out a CD that's not a rip off

Chapter 7

The desire to live righteously

What's Divine
Love, It's Just Love
The Man I Want To Be
It All Comes Around
Walls Of Shame
Motivational Blues
Just An Open Door

WHAT'S DIVINE

I'm just a lonely man
Searching for the Promised Land
What's behind the door?
Never seen before
Tell me if you see a plan

It may take many years
To discover why I have these fears
Will I be alone?
And my hopes all gone?
When time runs out on me

There's no way
Something can turn you away
It's okay
Others will always say
If you keep the question in mind
You will finally find what's divine
The truth behind the signs
The truth behind the signs

We're on this earth to lend a helping hand
To a man that finds it hard to stand
On his own two legs
And his heart it begs
For something to believe in

We'll take it to the top
Never let it be forgot
We have dignity
So we have to see
What's in store for us beyond our time

LOVE, ITS JUST LOVE

I want to love myself
When all my dreams are on the shelf
I'll still believe in myself
Can you tell?
I want to love someone else
Someone with a certain sense of self
Because when I'm old and poor in health
At least I won't be by myself

Love, love is all you need
Love, like destiny, a reality
Love, it's just love
Love, it's just love

You say you want to love yourself
You've got to take it off the shelf
You ought to give it to yourself
It's divine!
You say you want to love someone else
You've got to stop thinking about yourself
Because when you're old and poor in health
At least you won't be by yourself

Love, love is all you need
Love, like destiny, a reality
Love, it's just love
Love, it's just love
Love, love
Love, love

THE MAN I WANT TO BE

(Jake McCrea/Ben McCrea)

This life!
I don't know where it all went wrong
I think it's tearing me apart
So where do I run to now?
This world!
Is crashing down on me
And the mountains are so high
How will I get to the other side?

I don't know but I'm getting too old
I don't know but I'm getting too old
I don't know but I'm getting too old
To be the man I want to be

People!
Always try to cut me down
When I try to please
I know they think I'm just a clown
Hey!
All you out there giving looks
Looks that mock my pride
You'd better step aside

I'm not too old to carry this load
I'm not too old to carry this load
I'm not too old to carry this load
And be the man I want to be
The man I want to be

I guess I shouldn't get upset when people cut me down
I know they only wish that they could play the clown
From now and forth I'm going to look ahead
Watch out, I'm here, woken from the dead

JAKE MCCREA

IT ALL COMES AROUND

What place shall I reside?
Just a special place to hide
To you I will confide
Cause you're on my side
Cause you're on my side
I've walked the streets before
In search of any open door
But no one lent a hand
Gave me looks I could not stand
Looks I could not stand
So now it's up to me

Listen
These are the facts that you've been given
So if you're tired of living
Hold your breath until you're driven
It all comes around
It all comes around

No one likes to lose in life
Some don't like to sacrifice
I've been down that road before
Thought a lot beside the shore
Thought a lot beside the shore
Now I'm ready to face the facts
No more looking back
I always knew I wanted more
I should have made that stand before
I should have made that stand before
So now it's up to me

WALLS OF SHAME

Give me some hope for today
Just like the earth soaks up the fallen rain
And if you hurt that's okay
Because I know I sometimes feel the same way
You say you're a clown
And then you frown
You're just an actor behind a disguise
Then you laugh at me
When I say we're free
You're always tied up in simple goodbyes

We're all lonely
But we'll never live in walls of shame
Walls of shame

Please don't compromise yourself
To meet the greeds of somebody else
And if someone treats you bad
Don't be sad, just be glad you're alive
And when the going gets tough
When life is rough
Shrug your shoulders and keep moving on
It's a mystery
Why we all don't see
Life is precious and someday it's gone

MOTIVATIONAL BLUES

I want just one thing, nothing to do
When I have to do something, motivational blues
A feeling inside, I don't want to lose
But the feeling subsides, motivational blues

Motivation, Initiation
Let your mind explore
Determination, aspiration
Feel your spirit soar
I need energy, why am I so tired?
I hate apathy, so little to inspire

I'm walking in circles, don't want to choose
Thinking about nothing, motivational blues
I'm griped by signs, what shall I do?
Wasting my time, motivational blues

Motivation, evaluation
Say a prayer before the war
Determination, salutation
We will remember you for sure
I need energy, why am I so tired?
I want empathy to mold my desires

Motivation, exaltation
Is Christ behind the door?
Determination, expectation
He will judge the rich and the poor
I need energy, why am I so tired?
I'll give you all of me, my guitar is all that I'll require
Motivation, motivational blues
Motivation, motivational blues

JUST AN OPEN DOOR

I'm tired of the hurt of my fellow man
I'd like to change a lot if I could understand
Why some fall through the holes
When they lose the will to survive

I'm tired of the rich always getting their way
While the poor struggle day to day
It's time to turn a leaf on the fallen man
If we can

When the rain drops to the ground
And the sound echos through the town
I feel I'm lost in the train of thought
To be brought where the battles fought
So I see an end in sight
So I can stand and know what's right
No more tears anymore, and what for?
Just an open door, just an open door

I'm tired of the earth always taking abuse
We have to be careful about our use
Or we'll end up living in a waste land
Where a man can't get their demands

I'm tired of the wars that rage and kill
When it's in your home it's a bitter pill
Why can't we just get along?
And belong, and be strong

Chapter 8

Giving thanks and seeking redemption

Something Inside
Coffee And Cigarettes
Oh No, I Love You
Amends With You
Can Of Worms
Redemption Time
To The Lord I Pray

SOMETHING INSIDE

Wish in a way
That I could prove God sent His only Son
To deliver our souls
The immortal light in everyone

Wish in a way
That I could be the man you want me to become
From sinner to saint
Someone who believes in Kingdom Come

And there's someone I've got to be
And there's something I've got to do
And there's something inside for me
And there's something inside for you

Wish in a way
That I could see the good in everyone
And I believe
True evil thrives in only some

Wish in a way
That I could seize the day, Thy will be done
Spreading the news
Judgement Day is soon to come

And there's someone I've got to be
And there's something I've got to do
And there's something inside for me
And there's something inside for you

And there's something inside for me
And there's something inside for you
Yeah, there's something inside for me
And there's something inside for you

COFFEE AND CIGARETTES

Give me coffee and cigarettes and I'm content
When I rise in the morning or in any event
Coffee and cigarettes go hand in hand
Coffee and cigarettes are in high demand

Give me sweet Mary Jane, to ease my mind
When you desperately want to pass the time
My sweet Mary Jane, accompany me
Mary Jane's my destiny

Give me a guitar to write songs that inspire
When I'm motivated to put my feet to the fire
A guitar and chords is all I need
A guitar and a creative seed

Give me a pen and paper so I can impress
Something you haven't considered yet
A pen and paper to prove the divine
A pen and paper to expand your mind

Give me some food and shelter and it's a blessing
When you're on the street and life's a lesson
Food and shelter, from day to day
Food and shelter for all, I pray

Give me my family and some friends and I'll get by
When you're lost there's someone to confide
Family and friends that you can love
Family and friends and God above

Give me faith and redemption and I am relieved
When the good in oneself is hard to achieve
Faith and redemption through moments of doubt
Faith and redemption are what God cares about

OH NO, I LOVE YOU

Some things are hard to explain
Yeah, but maybe there not meant to be
Being in love is somehow the same
But it comes so naturally

The stars in the sky shine bright baby
It sets the mood for tonight
But in case you plan to run baby
Don't forget to write

Oh no, no, no
Oh no, I love you
Oh no, no, no
Oh no, I love you

I want to give you all of me
And I want you to belong
I know I've got the key
Please don't tell me that I'm wrong
I want to share my life with you
I know I can be strong
All my wicked ways are through
Please don't make me wait so long

The soul of the sky goes deep baby
The smile on your face won't deny
But if love ever leaves your heart baby
Don't forget to say goodbye

Oh no, no, no
Oh no, I love you
Oh no, no, no
Oh no, I love you

AMENDS WITH YOU

Believe in me
Cause I'm too weak to carry on
All my fears
Gather here
Inside this hollow shell
But I try
To get by
In spite of myself

Believe in me
Because I guess I'm not that strong
All I know
I bestow
To you in times of need
Now can you
See me through
My misery

And I try to escape
God knows I need a break in life
Now I know I must make
Amends with you, amends with you
Amends with you, amends with you

Believe in me
Cause I'll never let you down
When you're not there
I despair
Do you want to see me cry?
Love is strange
Cause I'm deranged
By the thoughts of you and I

CAN OF WORMS

Everyone has their can of worms
But we don't like to reveal it
With time we don't want to regret
Remember why we had to seal it
Forgive us Lord, we want what's good
Helping others like we should
Kindness goes a long way
And through meditation, and when we pray
We are like chunks of clay
In need of molding day to day

Like opening a can of worms
Too embarrassed to reveal
The guilt is more than I can take
More than I can feel
So take this can of worms
And throw it in the fire
So we can watch it burn
It's you that we admire

Everyone has their can of worms
Concealed in the past
But just as the world will learn
Keep your mind to the task
Forgive us Lord, for we have sinned
And heal this broken-hearted man
Lift this burden from my shoulders
And as time goes by and as I grow older
To you I will confess
Because it's you I want to impress

REDEMPTION TIME

All I want is some redemption
To get back to where I belong
People always make assumptions
It hurts to think they've got me wrong
All I need is some redemption
Now's the time to make it right
I know that I can mend the fences
In truth there is an end in sight

I'm seeking to achieve my best
I'm longing to ace the test
Redemption to prove I'm worthy
To make clean, what is dirty
Redemption time to clear my slate
Redemption time to end debate
Redemption time to reinvent
An image worth embodiment

All I long for is some redemption
A positive reflection of my love
Just hoping for a good reception
Giving thanks to God above
All I pray for is some redemption
Forgiveness for my sins
Help to avoid temptation
So destiny begins

I haven't always made the mark
But I've tried to take it all to heart
Redemption to erase the past
Into the fire my sins are cast
I resent the devil and all his crimes
I've spent some time with his grip on mine
Now it's time to deny his wrath
Get on the straight and narrow path
The future holds a better day
And I know redemption is on its way

TO THE LORD I PRAY

When something goes wrong, it's just a moment in time
When people grow old, it's just a state of mind
When you discover the signs from above
That's when the suffering is comforted by love

I can't recover all those lost years
But I can begin to live without fear
And when the angels come to take me away
Remember me, to the Lord I pray

When life gets hard to bare, it sometimes tests our faith
As days make us weary, we contemplate
But let there be no doubt, our destiny is sealed
Prophecies of the times are revealed

When I pray I'll think of you
When I say I feel the blues
I know you'll hold me and wipe my tears
All I've got to do is pray, and I know you'll hear

Chapter 9

Truth, prophecy, and the celebration of life

Write A Book Of Love
Jesus Will Save Me
Signs Of Life
The Prophecy
The Golden Years
My Little Girl
My Medicine Man

WRITE A BOOK OF LOVE

We're sons and daughters all the same
We're under pressure every day
And when we can't believe what may
We tend to drag about and say
I don't deserve to feel this way
I can't help struggle day to day
If you could only read my mind
You'd see I'm only steps behind,
Only steps behind,
You'd see I'm only steps behind

The earth it longs for peace to stay
The power of love is soon to reign
So when you go about your day
You'll know that love will find a way,
Love will find a way,
You'll know that love will find a way

Write! What's up above
Write! A book of love
I'm not kidding you, this song's ridding you
Of all the demons in your mind
It's time to change the path of time

The saints and prophets knew the score
I never felt this way before
I know there's a lot for me to write
The story of a stringless kite
Now I'm never holding back
And with the truth I will attack
Love is sacred to my book
Giving life an honest look,
Life's an honest look,
Giving life an honest look

JESUS WILL SAVE ME

There was a book of prophecy that never told
How the signs of the times they do unfold
We must look to God to identify
With all that's sacred, the connections in your life
I prayed at the Virgin Mary's shrine
I've walked the hills and travelled all my life
Just like those who search their soul
Now I've found I've got a greater role

Now I believe I've got an answer for my soul
Now I believe I've got a purpose to be told
Now I believe that things will work out right
Cause in my heart I'm too tired to fight

Jesus came to set the world straight
And if you believe in Him, there will be no debate
Cause in the end when you stare death in the eye
You'll realize what it means to be alive

Now I believe in the prophets throughout time
Now I believe in the saints and the signs
Now I believe things will work out right
Cause in my heart I'm too tired to fight
Jesus will save me
These things I'll always know
Jesus will save me
He wants every faithful soul
Jesus will save me
Jesus will save me
Jesus will save me

SIGNS OF LIFE

I see the signs of life
Inspire me and make me smile
My life is like a strange connection
My life is just another trial
I see the signs of life
Entertain me a while
My life in reckless abandon
My age in denial

You've got to judge your ways
And reconcile
You've got to live your life
Like a democratic trial

I see the signs of life
With every mistake I make
It's just one or the other
Will you forsake?
I see the signs of life
And I must make amends
Honesty, it ain't easy
But on this it depends

I see the signs of life speak loud and clear
Whispers of fortune approaching and near
I see the signs of life leading me on
Secrets of divine, and demonic in song

THE PROPHECY

Daniel 12: 3-4
And those who have insight will shine brightly
Like the brightness of the expanse of Heaven,
And those who lead the many to righteousness,
Like the stars forever and ever.
But for you Daniel, conceal the words
And seal up the book until the end of time.
Many will go back and forth, and knowledge will increase.

Have you ever thought you'd been there before?
Deja-vu or maybe a whole lot more
Seeing yourself in the sands of time
Serving the servant, changing water to wine
How did you feel?
Have you ever dreamt you could save the world?
Wrestle with angels, even a score
Or maybe you dreamt you were leading the masses
Into damnation like a modern day fascist
How did you feel? Can this be real?
When you read between the lines
Picking up on little signs

There's something familiar to open your mind
There's something peculiar in the sands of time
Don't you forget it, you won't regret it
Seek the truth and the truth you will find
Building a bridge between Heaven and Earth
Breaking the seal, breaking the curse
As we evolve, our souls will revolve
Open the door, a door to rebirth

It's all in how you read the signs
Maybe it's evil, maybe divine
Show me the way down life's lonely highway
Skipping your way, tripping down mine
But I've heard about 'The Book of Life'
And I wonder if we're in it
Oh Daniel did you break the seal?
And start a new beginning

How would you feel to reach your potential?
Use your uniqueness as a credential
Read the connections, some say coincidence
A man in reflection, a sign of deliverance
Can you believe? Will you receive?
When you read between the lines
Picking up on little signs

There's something familiar to open your mind
There's something peculiar in the sands of time
Don't you forget it, you won't regret it
Seek the truth and the truth you will find
Building a bridge between Heaven and Earth
Breaking the seal, breaking the curse
As we evolve our souls will revolve
Open the door, a door to rebirth
A door to rebirth
A door to rebirth

THE GOLDEN YEARS

May God bless all the years
That we may prosper in our lives
Every season come and gone
Admiring a spark
Still glowing red against the night
From a fire burning strong

May those you love remember you
Through the years, beyond that day
When the time, it fades away
And all your hopes of paradise
Reflect on yesterdays
Where true love led the way

Savor cheer, in the golden years, anniversary
Savor tear, in the golden years, anniversary

May all your children carry on
What you have taught them all along
Just like this sacrament of song
And when we think of two
We'll always think of you
And a love that is so strong

Savor cheer, in the golden years, anniversary
Savor tear, in the golden years, anniversary

It's the way, you take my heart away
When you say, your love will always stay
As a golden day

MY LITTLE GIRL

Dimples is my cat and she always wants to snuggle
Dimples is a fat cat so motivation is a struggle
Pig out my hairy little beast
Tonight's the night to have a feast
My cat gets nothing less than roast beef and chicken breast

My cat's a Persian, the kind I like!
I have a preference despite
Her squished nose and black lipstick
She's cuter than a newborn is!
Oh! Dimple-ee-pooh
Come to Dad my little girl!
Oh! Dimple-ee-pooh
Let's take on the world!

Dimples is old at 17, but she never looked better
But knowing fate is bound in chains, she won't live forever
So when the time is right to leave this world
You'll always remain my special girl
My cat gets nothing less than a permanent address

Yeah, Dimples is my cat, that's just a matter of fact
And this is what it's like for Dimples in her life
She gets treats for her affection
She gets her belly scratched upon her direction
She loves her Dad and treats him well, a little trooper purring pal
She does her duty in the box, and she likes to sniff her master's socks
She loves to snuggle night and day, and he likes to comb her knots away
She lets him know everything's fine, and knows he'll always have the time
Sleeping is Dimple's favorite though
So sleep my girl, through life we go

MY MEDICINE MAN

Things aren't so bad I guess
He gave me escape from the abyss
I'm glad to have known him too
He was always there to care about you
I used to love the time we spent
Discussing life's current events
We always found common ground
To me he was the lost and found

I've never known someone this way
A visionary in our time
Built me a bridge from day to day
And gave me peace of mind
With his trademark smile
He was always there to brighten your day
This was just his style
He just had a certain way

He always left me feeling I could
Cope with the changes in life like I should
Easing my mind with a pen and paper
Just getting to know me better
But to me he was more than a man of science
To me he was a friend
And though he didn't rely on signs
Because of him I'm on the mend

He always listened to me express
Fears in my life, I'd try to impress
His wisdom and wit helped me along
Through the crossroads of life, and then some
He was a pleasure most of the time
Enjoyed his pipe and fine cheap wines
Yeah, he was an original guy
It makes it hard to say goodbye

He listened, he cared
In my life he shared
Was honest and kind
Always had the time
He freed me, believed me
Of all that he heard
Someone to confide to
A man of his word
I will remember, my medicine man
I will remember, my medicine man

Author Biography

Jake McCrea grew up along-side three brothers, nurtured by two loving parents. He is the second oldest brother, and probably 'the wildest of the bunch', according to his father. He completed a BSC degree at the University of Saskatchewan with plans to go into the health care field. When things didn't pan out for him he moved to the west coast to pursue a music career.

Jake picked up the guitar after a European adventure in 1989-90 and started writing songs shortly after. He lived in Vancouver for a couple of years. There he immersed himself in the music scene; jamming with other musicians, performing at open stages, and busking to supplement his living. Jake continued to write and made a few recordings during his years in Vancouver.

Following his return to Saskatoon Jake recorded a series of demo albums, which he used to get gigs and promote his music. In 1998 he came out with a self-titled demo album of old recordings; songs recorded in Saskatoon as well as some recordings from his time in Vancouver. He sold this CD exclusively to friends and family.

Jake followed this up with several other releases. The most memorable was probably 'The Golden Crossroads' demo in 2001. Jake has rereleased this CD to coincide with the launch of this book of poetry and songs. He has written a wealth of new material over a span of three decades, some of which are published in this book.

Jake continues to write and is working on a novel centered around his experience at the crossroads in Golden, B.C., and the ensuing events, and how they shaped his faith and destiny. He also tells his interpretation of this mysterious journey through his music and poetry. Jake is actively doing gigs and poetry readings whenever he gets the chance. He resides in Saskatoon with his two black Persian cats.

Printed in Canada